Original title:
Overcoming Challenges

Copyright © 2024 Swan Charm
All rights reserved.

Editor: Jessica Elisabeth Luik
Author: Sara Säde
ISBN HARDBACK: 978-9916-86-533-0
ISBN PAPERBACK: 978-9916-86-534-7

Illuminated Pathways

Beneath the starry night, a road so clear,
With whispers of the wind that guide the way.
Each step a dance, where shadows disappear,
In moonlight's grace, the dark and light both play.

Ancient trees loom tall, their secrets deep,
Offering their wisdom in soft hums.
Leaves rustle tales that forest spirits keep,
As silent echoes beat like nature's drums.

A creek winds gently, sparkling in the glow,
Reflecting dreams that shimmer in the stream.
It sings a song from ages long ago,
Where hopes and fantasies entwine and gleam.

The scent of pine, so earthy and so true,
Invokes the essence of a world so old.
A journey painted in each breath we drew,
With footsteps marking stories left untold.

Each star above, a beacon in the vast,
Guiding hearts through realms unknown and wide.
Illuminated pathways draw us past,
To worlds where dreams and reality collide.

Unyielding Spirit

Through paths of thorns and skies so grey,
With resolute heart, I find my way.
In every storm, through endless night,
My spirit soars, an unquenched light.

Beneath the weight of deepest fears,
I forge ahead, dry my tears.
Where shadows loom and doubts collide,
Strength and hope walk by my side.

In trials' grasp, where others fall,
I stand my ground and heed the call.
For every dawn that breaks anew,
A testament to what I pursue.

Breaking Chains

Forged in darkness, bound by steel,
Shackles tight, I refuse to kneel.
With every cry, with every strain,
I dream anew of breaking chain.

Within my soul, a fire burns bright,
To taste the day and feel the light.
In freedom's name, I give my all,
To rise and stand, to never fall.

The echoes of a shackled past,
Are drowned by dreams that grow so vast.
For with each step towards the free,
I claim my right, my destiny.

In the Face of Odds

When shadows fall, when hopes are thin,
I find the strength to fight within.
Against the odds, through weary days,
I blaze a path with endless praise.

Through skeptic eyes and daunting stares,
I rise above the world's despairs.
With faith unbroken, heart profound,
I shatter walls and break new ground.

For every challenge, fierce and grand,
I face the storm with outstretched hand.
In the face of odds, where courage blooms,
I write my fate amongst the moons.

Path of Persistence

Upon this road, where shadows creak,
We tread with hearts that firmly speak.
Enduring trials, our spirits soar,
Through storm and rain, we seek the shore.

Each step we take, though weight may grow,
We gather strength from what we know.
The path is long, but not in vain,
For after night comes light again.

In valleys deep and mountains high,
We raise our dreams unto the sky.
With every fall and rise anew,
The path of persistence, we pursue.

Resilient Souls

Through winds that howl and waves that crash,
Our souls withstand each roaring lash.
With courage bound in every thread,
We face the dawns that lie ahead.

Against the tide, we hold our ground,
In every loss, new hope is found.
The scars we bear, they tell a tale,
Of hearts that fight and never pale.

As seasons change, our roots dig deep,
In nurturing the dreams we keep.
Through summer's blaze, and winter's frost,
Resilient souls are never lost.

To the Peak

Upon the slopes where eagles fly,
We set our gaze where peak meets sky.
With every breath and every stride,
Mountains yield to those with pride.

The rocks may harsh, the air be thin,
Yet perseverance wears the grin.
Through mists that veil the summit's grace,
We climb with hope and steady pace.

In echoes of the winds that scream,
Reside the whispers of our dream.
To reach the top where vistas gleam,
We forge ahead, a steadfast team.

Survivor's Song

In shadows cast by fateful hands,
Resilience breathes where despair stands,
Wounds of time may scar the skin,
But strength is found deep within.

Beneath the weight, the spirit soars,
Through broken dreams and unclosed doors,
Courage whispers in the night,
A hopeful heart in the darkest fight.

Each dawn arrives to heal the fray,
With gentle light to guide the way,
In battle's wake, the soul renews,
A warrior's song in vibrant hues.

Dark to Light

In shadows cast by moonless night,
We searched for dawn, a glimmer bright.
Through thickened gloom and creeping fears,
We held our light against the tears.

With trembling hands, we pierced the veil,
Where darkness sought to weave its tale.
A spark within, a guiding star,
Led us to realms both near and far.

Emerging from the deepest shade,
We found the dawn of hopes remade.
From dark to light, the journey calls,
To rise beyond the shadowed walls.

Braving the Void

In a sea of endless night,
We chart our course unknown,
Through stars that gleam so bright,
In worlds unseen, alone.

With hearts that dare to dream,
We sail on waves of air,
In realms where shadows gleam,
And whispers dare not share.

Embrace the boundless space,
With courage, pierce the gloom,
In every darkened place,
New galaxies will bloom.

Through voids that seem to swallow,
Our spirit glows so bright,
We brave the dark to follow,
The dreamers' guiding light.

In mysteries vast and deep,
Our souls forever roam,
In voids we bravely leap,
And make the stars our home.

Eclipsing Shadows

In twilight's soft embrace,
The shadows come to play,
They dance with quiet grace,
Eclipse the light of day.

A whisper on the breeze,
A secret left untold,
In shadows, mysteries,
In darkness, stories unfold.

The moon's a silver ghost,
A beacon in the night,
It shadows all we boast,
Yet fills us with its light.

In every shadow cast,
A promise to be found,
The present, future, past,
In darkness, all are bound.

Eclipsing shadows wane,
Yet never truly fade,
In light we find the same,
And learn from every shade.

Bridges to Tomorrow

Across the gulf of time and space,
We build the future's saving grace,
With every beam and trust bestowed,
A bridge to dreams where hope is sowed.

Through trials past and sorrows borne,
A path to dawn, anew, reborn,
Hand in hand, we cast our fears,
And walk towards the coming years.

In unity, foundations lie,
A testament beneath the sky,
With courage strong and vision clear,
We shape the world, frontier to near.

Steadfast Hearts

In fields where tempests rise,
And skies are dark and grey,
Our hearts with steadfast ties,
Will guide us on our way.

Through storms we shall not falter,
With courage as our guide,
Our spirits will not alter,
Together we abide.

In trials that we face,
And fears that we must fight,
With love's enduring grace,
We find our inner light.

No force can break or tear,
The bond that we possess,
In every joy and care,
Our hearts remain steadfast.

Through every night and day,
In laughter, pain, and trials,
We'll walk the steadfast way,
Together, all the miles.

Blaze of Honor

In the dawn's first golden gleam,
A herald of the flame,
We rise with honor's dream,
And play the valiant game.

With courage as our spear,
And truth as our shield,
In every heart sincere,
To pride we never yield.

In battles fierce and wide,
Our banners bold and bright,
We carry deep inside,
A blaze of honor's light.

Through victory and loss,
We stand with heads held high,
On pathways that we cross,
Our honor never dies.

A blaze that will endure,
In every heart and hand,
With honor strong and pure,
Together we shall stand.

The Path Through Peaks

Among the hills where silence speaks,
A journey starts, the path through peaks,
With every step, a vista grand,
The mountains whisper, hand in hand.

Clouds embrace the towering crest,
In nature's arms, the weary rest,
An echo sings of ancient lore,
In valleys deep and evermore.

Through bramble fields and rocky rise,
The soul ascends to meet the skies,
In heights of peace, the spirit gleams,
The heart is free in lofty dreams.

Incandescent Fortitude

Through flames of trial, the steel is forged,
In heat and pressure, courage surged,
A beacon bright 'midst storm and dark,
Incandescent, fierce, and stark.

The will to stand when shadows fall,
Unyielding heart through every squall,
A lantern burns within the chest,
A guiding light in nights oppressed.

With every challenge, strength refines,
The soul's resolve in brilliant lines,
Fortitude's fire, forever bright,
An inner sun, defying night.

Courage in Silence

In the quiet, strength does bloom,
A whisper cutting through the gloom,
Unafraid of shadows' plight,
It holds firm in endless night.

Voices gentle, hearts are grand,
Braving seas with steadfast hand,
No need for shouts or loud acclaim,
In silence lives a hero's name.

Through the whisper, through the calm,
Peace is found in courage's palm,
Not by might, but by resolve,
Silent strength the key to solve.

Faces stern, yet souls are kind,
Speak with heart, not just with mind,
Pure courage needs no bolstering sound,
In soft repose, the brave are found.

Enduring Flame

Through the winds and through the rain,
Burns a flame immune to pain,
Yearning with a fiery soul,
Guided by an unseen goal.

Not for dimness, not for fear,
But for light it holds dear,
Burning bright in every storm,
Keeping all that's pure, warm.

In the ashes, rise anew,
With a strength none ever knew,
An enduring flame alights,
All the world with glowing sights.

Flickers soft yet firm and true,
Blazes forth with passion's hue,
Eternal, bright, and never tame,
Such is life's enduring flame.

Light in the Abyss

Deep below where shadows trace,
Glimmer sparks in moonlit grace,
Light emerges from the dark,
Hope ignites with steadfast spark.

Lost in depths of endless night,
Faintest glow becomes a sight,
Through the murk and jagged path,
Radiance dispels the wrath.

Guiding hands with gentle hue,
Brightens eyes with dreams anew,
In the chasm, love unkissed,
Finds its way, a light amidst.

Unknown worlds that blaze within,
Lit by courage, not by sin,
In the heart's abyssal hold,
Shines a story yet untold.

Boundless Horizons

In the vast expanse of azure skies,
Where dreams take flight and spirits rise,
Whispers of the wind call us forth,
To chase the endless, boundless worth.

Mountains high and valleys deep,
Guard the secrets we strive to keep,
With every step, a tale untold,
Horizons vast, adventures bold.

Stars above and fields below,
Guiding lights where shadows grow,
We'll wander far with hearts elate,
In horizon's arms, we seal our fate.

Scars and Sunshine

Lines that mark a journey's end,
Trace the battles fought within,
Every scar a testament,
To the sunlight that begins.

Wounds may heal but tales do last,
In the shadows of the past,
Where the light has kissed the pain,
Brings the sunshine after rain.

Fading colors, echo cries,
In the morning, daybreak lies,
Stars that pierce the night-time veil,
Guide the heart through wind and wail.

Bright and dark in fusion grand,
Craft the soul with gentle hand,
Scars and sunshine intertwined,
Form a life, uniquely kind.

Emergence of Hope

From depths of night, a dawn will break,
Through shadows dark, a light will wake,
Whispers soft of morning's grace,
Hope emerges, finds its place.

In hearts that faltered, strength is born,
From seeds of doubt, resilience torn,
With every tear a promise spun,
In hope's embrace, a new day's sun.

Through storms that rage and winds that wail,
In hope's strong arms, we shall prevail,
For in the darkest, loneliest night,
Hope's gentle flame will shine so bright.

Wings of Determination

In the stillness of a silent prayer,
With wings unseen, we cut through air,
Eyes fixed on dreams but miles away,
Determined hearts shall find their way.

Across the valleys of despair,
Through trials harsh and fields unfair,
Our wings of will shall lift us high,
To touch the stars that line the sky.

Though doubts may cloud and paths confound,
In determination, we're unbound,
For every step and every leap,
Our wings shall soar, no bounds they'll keep.

The Infinite Climb

Upon the slopes where shadows play,
We carve our paths, we find our way,
Each summit near reveals the climb,
An endless dance, defying time.

The rocks beneath, the sky above,
Whisper tales of courage, love,
With each ascent, our spirits grow,
In the infinite climb, we come to know.

No peak too high, no depth too wide,
In every fall, a strength inside,
We rise again with hearts so prime,
In the boundless, infinite climb.

Heart of Steel

In a world of fleeting days,
Strength remains through night and haze,
Guided by an inner zeal,
Behold the heart, a core of steel.

Dreams may falter, slip, and fade,
But resolve is never swayed,
Faced with trials, unyielding might,
Shining through the darkest night.

With every challenge bravely met,
Courage we shall not forget,
A beacon in the storm's appeal,
Standing strong with heart of steel.

Whispers of the past may call,
Echoes in the endless hall,
Yet forward steps we boldly take,
Hearts of steel will never break.

So forge ahead, the path revealed,
Guard the fire, hearts annealed,
In the end, the truth we seal,
Victory to the heart of steel.

Defying Gravity

Skyward bound, we break the chains,
Beyond the clouds, defying pains,
Above the earth, in free ascent,
Boundless dreams, our firmament.

With whispered winds and wings so wide,
We soar on currents, free to glide,
Each breathless leap a bold decree,
In endless blue, we're truly free.

Knowing not what lies above,
With every rise, a test of love,
Hearts alight with fiery flare,
Defying gravity, we dare.

Eclipsing fears, we start to climb,
Unconfined by space or time,
Together in this vast expanse,
We find our flight, we take our chance.

Lifted by the light unseen,
Held by hope, our spirits keen,
We transcend, with hearts so brave,
Defying gravity, we pave.

The Resilient Heart

Through the storms and through the rain,
Bearing loss, enduring pain,
There within, a fire starts,
A testament, the resilient heart.

Bent but broken, never falls,
Echoing in empty halls,
Rising through the deepest dark,
Guided by a radiant spark.

Every wound a whispered scar,
Mapping journeys traveled far,
With each beat, a brand new start,
Pledging to the resilient heart.

In the face of doubt and fear,
Stronger still with every tear,
It rebuilds, a work of art,
Built by hands of the resilient heart.

Standing tall through every trial,
Onward with a measured smile,
Endlessly, we'll never part,
In unity, the resilient heart.

Winged Resolve

Far above the earthly tether,
Bound by neither chain nor weather,
Spirits lifted, sights absolve,
Onward with a winged resolve.

As the dawn ignites the skies,
Hope within us starts to rise,
Every heartbeat, bold, involved,
Guided by our winged resolve.

Crossing vast celestial plains,
Freedom courses through our veins,
With each gust, our fears dissolve,
Strengthened by a winged resolve.

Through the tempests, through the gales,
In our essence, it prevails,
Always pushing to evolve,
Driven by our winged resolve.

Ever forward in our quest,
With each trial, we stand the test,
Boundless dreams that we resolve,
Taking flight with winged resolve.

Temple of Strength

In walls of stone, the echoes sing,
A story of courage, an eternal spring.
Each pillar holds the weight of time,
A testament to the heart's own chime.

Through trials faced and battles won,
The temple shines like the morning sun.
Strength is built with every scar,
Guiding us where heroes are.

Beneath the sky so vast and grand,
Against the odds, together we stand.
Our spirits fused in unity,
Creating a fortress of divinity.

In every struggle, an inner light,
Leads us through the darkest night.
Brick by brick, we rise anew,
Crafting temples, firm and true.

With every step, a legacy forged,
In hearts where bravery is stored.
The temple stands, a beacon bright,
Defining strength in endless light.

Path Unbroken

On roads less traveled, paths untold,
A journey of the brave and bold.
Steps of faith in shadows cast,
Walking forward, steadfast at last.

With every twist and turn we find,
The strength of heart, the power of mind.
Terrain may challenge, skies may gray,
Yet, on this path, we choose to stay.

The weight of doubts, the miles unbending,
Dreams of flight are never-ending.
Hope alight, we march along,
For in our soul the journey's song.

In every footfall, courage gleams,
As we pursue our distant dreams.
A path unbroken, paved with fight,
Guided by an inner light.

Through valleys deep and mountains high,
We see the world through clear blue sky.
Our journey molds us, shapes our core,
A path unbroken forevermore.

Stronger Winds

Whispers in the breeze so soft,
Turn to howls that lift us aloft.
Stronger winds that shape our fate,
Throughout the storms, we never abate.

Each gust brings forth a lesson learned,
In hearts where fires of courage burned.
Stronger winds may bend the tree,
But roots hold firm in unity.

In battles waged against the night,
We find our strength, we find our light.
Struggling winds may test our might,
Yet in their sway, we find our flight.

With every storm, we rise anew,
Resilient spirits breaking through.
Embracing gusts that shape and form,
Emerging calm after the storm.

Stronger winds that bend and blend,
Forge the spirit, help hearts mend.
Standing tall, we face the gale,
In stronger winds, we will prevail.

Embers of Fortitude

From ashes cold, a fire ascends,
A beacon bright where darkness ends.
With hearts ablaze, they brave the fight,
Embers of fortitude, burning bright.

In quiet moments, strength revealed,
Through trials faced, their fate is sealed.
Resilient hearts that dreams unbind,
Embers of fortitude, souls aligned.

Across the winds, their whispers fly,
Defying gloom, reaching high.
Unyielding flame in every stare,
Embers of fortitude, everywhere.

Resilience Unfolded

Within us lies a hidden fire,
Fanning flames of fierce desire.
In every trial, our spirits tested,
In resilience, our hearts are vested.

With every fall, we rise once more,
Stronger than we were before.
Bound by trials, yet unbroken,
Resilience in every token.

Beneath the weight, our hearts are bold,
A story of resilience unfolded.
Each chapter written in hardship's ink,
In every trial, we bravely sink.

In storms we find our deeper strength,
Through shadows go to any length.
Resilience crafted in life's forge,
In adversity, our spirits gorge.

From every hardship, courage springs,
Unfolding resilience on mighty wings.
With hearts unyielding, spirits bright,
We conquer darkness with endless light.

Warrior's Resolve

In shadows deep, where battles crawl,
A warrior's cry, defies the night,
Through storm and flame, he stands tall,
His spirit burning, fierce and bright.

Armor cracked and vision blurred,
Yet onward pushes, heart unbowed,
For every wound, a valor stirred,
In silence strong, he pledges loud.

Through mire and frost, on paths unknown,
No fear can tether, no doubt can bind,
For in his chest, a fire is sown,
A warrior's soul, of dauntless kind.

Eyes ablaze with starlit scheme,
Each step a testament to might,
He carves his fate, a vivid dream,
In dawn's embrace, dispelling night.

When twilight falls, on fields once red,
The warrior stands, with battles won,
His legend grown, by courage fed,
A beacon bright, until life's done.

Rise from the Ruins

From ashes grey, new spirits form,
In ruins cold, where hope once died,
The heartbeats spark in rhythmic norm,
As strength and will resurge the tide.

In broken lands where shadows creep,
A whisper threads through crumbled walls,
Awakening dreams from restless sleep,
As courage kneels but never falls.

Through rubble, loss, and silent cries,
Resilient sparks ignite anew,
The scarred earth smiles with starry eyes,
As dawn bestows a golden hue.

From fractured past, they rise once more,
Each step a vow to never yield,
In unity, their spirits soar,
A mighty song across the field.

For even as the ruins lie,
The seeds of hope forever bloom,
And from the dark, their spirits fly,
To brighter worlds, beyond the gloom.

The Strength to Rise

Amid the trials, where shadows feast,
The strength within begins to bloom,
A whisper soft, a roar unleashed,
Dispelling dread and fall's dark gloom.

With every step through valleys grim,
The heart learns lessons deep and true,
For light within, it cannot dim,
With every fall, it starts anew.

Beneath the storm and howl of night,
A beacon bright, a spirit keen,
To rise above with will and might,
The soul unbound, forever clean.

In trials fierce, where doubt may glare,
Resilience forms in steadfast grace,
A power felt, beyond compare,
To shape and mold a brighter space.

So, rise anew, with courage pure,
For strength within shall light the way,
Through darkest nights, it shall endure,
To guide you to a brighter day.

Hearts Against the Gale

In fierce winds where the storms reside,
Hearts gather strength, a force so rare,
With every gust, they will abide,
Their courage bold, beyond compare.

The gale may howl and thunder roar,
Yet hearts stand firm, unbroken, true,
Against the tempest, they implore,
A bond of steel, through skies of blue.

With whispered vows, they stake their claim,
In unity, they forge their path,
No storm can quench their burning flame,
Or thwart their will, their righteous wrath.

For in the dawn, as mist recedes,
Their shapes emerge, a steadfast line,
Through trials fought, they've sown the seeds,
Of hope and strength, a love divine.

Thus, hearts against the gale refrain,
In unison, they face the storm,
With every breach, they rise again,
Together bound, in spirit warm.

Silent Warriors

In shadows deep, they forge their path,
Stealthy footfalls tread the past.
With courage hued by silent might,
They guard the day, embrace the night.

Unseen by eyes, they stand the test,
Against the odds, they give their best.
Beneath the stars, their spirits climb,
Silent warriors, outlasting time.

Through battles harsh, through storms untold,
Their hearts beat strong, unwavering bold.
In whispers soft, their legends grow,
Silent warriors, their strength we know.

Undaunted Journey

Through paths uncharted, we tread with grace,
Hearts unyielding, we find our place.
Mountains high, and valleys low,
In every step, our spirits grow.

With courage as our guiding light,
We traverse the darkest night.
Against the odds, we rise and fight,
Dreams ignited, burning bright.

In shadows deep, the sun shall break,
A new dawn rising, for our sake.
Boundless skies, our aspirations take,
A journey bold, no fear, no quake.

Through trials fierce, we stand our ground,
In silence, strength resounds profound.
Echoes of resilience, all around,
In victory, our names are crowned.

From start to end, an endless quest,
Each step we take, proves us the best.
In every heart, the will to invest,
The undaunted journey, we manifest.

Flames of Perseverance

Amidst the heat, we stand our way,
In burning trials, we shall not sway.
Flames of struggle, night and day,
In perseverance, our hope will stay.

Through fiery storms, we forge ahead,
With hearts unbroken, never dread.
Bound by hopes, our spirits led,
In every ember, courage bred.

The fire burns, yet fuels our might,
In darkest hours, shines the light.
Against the flames, we stand upright,
Unyielding spirits, burning bright.

From ashes rise, in strength profound,
With every step, our truths are found.
In perseverance, our dreams unbound,
Through every trial, our hearts resound.

In every blaze, a lesson learned,
With every spark, our passions burned.
In perseverance, our souls affirmed,
The flames of life, we have discerned.

Holding On to Hope

In times of doubt, we hold on tight,
To hope eternal, shining bright.
Though shadows stretch as day turns night,
Our faith unbroken, in the light.

Through storms of life, we hold our ground,
With every step, resilience found.
In whispered winds, a hopeful sound,
In hearts of steel, our dreams are bound.

As dark clouds gather, we remain,
In hope, we find the strength to gain.
Though trials test and bring us pain,
In hope, our spirits unchained.

Within each tear, a seed of grace,
In every sorrow, hope we chase.
Through every struggle we embrace,
In hope's warm cradle, find our place.

Against the odds, we won't despair,
With hopeful hearts, beyond compare.
In hope we trust, in hope we dare,
As dreams take flight on wings of air.

Waves of Determination

In waves unyielding, we set our course,
Determined hearts, a mighty force.
Against the tide, with no remorse,
In every wave, we find our source.

Through tempests fierce, we make our way,
In surging seas, we do not sway.
With every crest, our hopes convey,
In determination, night and day.

Each wave we take, a test of will,
Through ebb and flow, we conquer still.
With steadfast hearts, our fears we kill,
In waves of strength, we climb each hill.

Against the current, we prevail,
In storms of life, we shall not fail.
With courage strong, we set our sail,
In waves of hope, our dreams unveil.

In endless surge, we find our peace,
In tides of life, our strength increase.
With every wave, our spirits cease,
In determination, we find release.

Rays of Tenacity

Amidst the clouds, through storm and haze,
Their light persists, in countless ways.
Bright rays of hope that never wane,
Rays of tenacity, break the chain.

With every dawn, a promise new,
To rise again, to journey through.
Their eyes reflect the morning sun,
Rays of tenacity, battles won.

Through tear-streaked nights and weary days,
Their strength endures, in myriad ways.
In every heart, a fire ignites,
Rays of tenacity, shining lights.

In the Face of Adversity

When shadows loom and hope seems thin,
They find the strength to rise within.
Defying fate with every breath,
In the face of adversity, they conquer death.

Their spirits soar where others fall,
With unbreakable will, they heed the call.
In darkest times, they forge their way,
In the face of adversity, they stay.

Through broken dreams and hearts so sore,
They stand as one and strive for more.
In each defeat, their victories lie,
In the face of adversity, they never die.

Beyond the Breaker

Where the waves meet sky and sea,
Dreams unfurl their sails so free.
Horizons kiss a golden hue,
Beckoning souls to venture through.

Mysteries lie beyond our reach,
Whispers in the salt and beach.
A world awaits beneath the crest,
Where weary hearts might find their rest.

Foam and spray caress the skin,
Amidst the roar, a calm within.
Beyond the breaker lies the key,
To a life less chained, eternally.

Unfurled Wings

In dawn's first light, wings catch the breeze,
A heart unbound, with dreams to seize.
From peak to plain, the journey starts,
In whispered winds, we find our parts.

With every beat, new heights are won,
Beneath the vast, eternal sun.
The sky, a canvas, pure and bright,
Painted with courage, fearless flight.

No chains can bind what's born to soar,
No earthly tether can implore.
To land and nest, a fleeting thing,
For evermore, we're unfurled wings.

Against the Tide

Upon the shore, where waves collide,
We dare to stand, against the tide.
With every surge, resolve swells too,
To face the challenge, break on through.

The currents push, intentions sway,
Yet in our hearts, bright faith will stay.
Against the tide, we find our strength,
Unyielding paths, through oceans' length.

In storm and calm, we stake our claim,
To live and strive, through joy and blame.
For in resistance, life's defined,
Against the tide, our souls aligned.

Silent Victories

In battles quiet, unseen fields,
We armor up, our spirit shields.
Through silent trials, the heart sustains,
In whispered strength, true power reigns.

No trumpets blare our valiant fight,
Yet in the shadows, darkness bright.
With every breath, resilience grows,
Silent victories, in ebb and flow.

For in the hush of night's embrace,
We conquer fears, with gentle grace.
In stillness found, our triumphs gleam,
Silent victories, a quiet dream.

Through the Fire

In the heart of infernos, we stride,
With courage and strength as our guide.
Through embers and flames, we persist,
In the dance of the fire, we exist.

The night, a canvas of despair,
Yet hope glimmers in the heated air.
With every step, we rise anew,
Through the fire, conquering the blue.

A phoenix from ashes, we become,
The past burns, but we overcome.
In the blaze, we find our name,
Through the fire, igniting our flame.

Golden sparks light up the dark,
In each ember, a destined mark.
Through trials fierce and dire,
We are forged, tempered in fire.

Beneath the molten, we uncover,
Strength unknown, like no other.
Through the fire, our spirits soar,
An eternal flame, forevermore.

Ascending Heights

In shadows deep, our journey starts,
With dreams aloft and fearless hearts.
Scaling cliffs, reaching for the sky,
With every step, we aim to fly.

Beneath the stars, the winds do sigh,
As we ascend, ever so high.
Mountains yield to our iron will,
Every summit, a newfound thrill.

Over crests, through valleys low,
Forward with an endless glow.
Each ascent, a whispered prayer,
Guiding us through thin mountain air.

With resolve as firm as stone,
In heights unknown, we find our home.
Against the odds, we rise above,
With fierce tenacity and boundless love.

To the peaks where eagles soar,
We climb, our spirits to explore.
Ascending heights, our souls ignite,
A testament to boundless might.

Boundless Courage

In the heart of daunting night,
We face the shadows, embrace the fight.
With courage boundless, spirits bright,
We march unwavering into the light.

Every challenge, a story told,
Of hearts so brave, of spirits bold.
Through tempest fierce and waters cold,
With boundless courage, we uphold.

The whispers of doubt may come and go,
But through the struggle, our valor grows.
In battles fought and victories sown,
Boundless courage stands alone.

From depths of fear, we find our call,
To rise above, to never fall.
Like lions, we face the world's expanse,
With boundless courage in our stance.

In every heart, a fire burns,
Through every path, our strength returns.
Boundless courage lights the way,
A guiding star in skies of grey.

Echoes of Triumph

In silence cold, where echoes dwell,
Lies the tale we yearn to tell.
Of battles fought and victories sound,
In echoes of triumph, we are found.

Through struggles fierce, dreams are spun,
In every heart, a war is won.
Across horizons far and wide,
Echoes of triumph, on every tide.

Among the stars, our hopes align,
With every whisper, a distant sign.
Through valleys deep and peaks so high,
Echoes of triumph reach the sky.

In every tear, a story gleams,
Of daring hopes and endless dreams.
Through shadows dark, we rise again,
Echoes of triumph, our refrain.

With strength untamed, we chase the dawn,
In every heartbeat, struggles gone.
Echoes of triumph, loud and clear,
A symphony we hold so dear.

Beyond the Storm

The clouds rolled in with mighty force,
The winds, they wailed, a wild discourse.
But hearts stood firm and spirits high,
We knew we'd see the clearer sky.

Raindrops danced upon the earth,
Each one a bearer of rebirth.
Lightning flashed, then faded fast,
Revealing hope that too shall last.

Mountains bowed to thunder's call,
Yet we remained, refusing fall.
Through the tempest, voices strong,
We found our place where we belong.

Embracing Dawn

The night retreats, and shadows fade,
The stars dissolve, their roles well played.
A hush, a breath of morning's grace,
As golden light begins its chase.

Birds awaken, songs anew,
In fields adorned with morning dew.
The world reborn with each new day,
In dawn's embrace, we find our way.

Mountains kiss the rising sun,
A promise kept, a race well run.
In twilight's soft and gentle yawn,
We greet the day, embracing dawn.

The Summit Awaits

A path through woods, by rivers wide,
Where secrets of the earth abide.
With every step, the summit calls,
Beyond the trees, the mountain tall.

Breath by breath, we rise and climb,
Through rugged trails and tests of time.
The sky, it broadens, azure bright,
A beacon in our onward flight.

Upon the peak, the world below,
A testament to all we know.
In reaching heights, our spirits say,
The summit waits to show the way.

Through the Dark

In shadows deep, we tread our way,
Through nights that stretch, devoid of day.
With faith as guide and heart as spark,
We journey on, through worlds so stark.

The stars above, our silent guides,
They watch as human hope abides.
Each step a leap, each breath a mark,
In endless quest, through the dark.

Hand in hand, we forge ahead,
With dreams of dawn where hope is fed.
For in the black, there lies a light,
That leads us through the darkest night.

Rise Above the Storm

The skies may roar, the winds may call,
A tempest fierce, it tries to stall,
But through the gale, we stand up tall,
And face the storm to never fall.

With every wave that crashes near,
We hold our ground, dismiss the fear,
For after tumult, skies grow clear,
And show the light to reappear.

In trials' wake, our hearts align,
We find our strength, a will divine,
Together through the strife, we shine,
And in the storm, our souls refine.

Whispers of Resilience

In whispered winds, a story spun,
Of battles fought and victories won,
Through quiet nights and blazing sun,
Resilience blooms, a force begun.

When shadows stretch and hopes grow thin,
A muster deep beneath the skin,
A call to rise from deep within,
A strength unknown will then begin.

The whispers speak of trials past,
Of mountains scaled and shadows cast,
In every heart the die is cast,
Resilience whispers, strong and fast.

Strength in the Shadows

In shadows deep where fears reside,
A quiet strength begins to bide,
Unseen in depths where doubts abide,
A will to rise, we will decide.

When nights grow long and paths obscure,
In darkness, we become more pure,
A hope that's hidden yet so sure,
In every shadow, strength mature.

From ashes cold, where embers lay,
A spark of hope will light the way,
In shadows, we no longer sway,
Our strength revealed in break of day.

Through the Ashes

When fires rage and skies grow dark,
And dreams lie buried, cold and stark,
In silent soot, a hopeful spark,
Through ashes gray, we'll leave our mark.

From ruins rise a will so strong,
It turns to right what once was wrong,
In every heart, a steadfast song,
Through endless night, we'll still belong.

The future calls through mists of gray,
A promise made to light our way,
We'll rise again, come what may,
Through ashes, dawn, a new born day.

Courageous Journey

Upon the path of stones and light,
We venture forth into the night.
With hearts of courage, minds so bright,
We chase our dreams, our goals in sight.

The winds may howl, the rain may fall,
But we stand firm, we heed the call.
With every step, we grow so tall,
In unity, we conquer all.

Through valleys deep and mountains high,
Our spirits soar, reaching the sky.
With every dawn, we ask not why,
But how to spread our wings and fly.

Each challenge faced, each lesson learned,
Our inner fires forever burned.
With every twist and every turn,
A bold new path we shall discern.

Fear not the shadows left behind,
For in our hearts, the light we find.
With courage true and love combined,
Our journey's end, a fate resigned.

Across the Abyss

A chasm wide, a daunting sight,
With darkness deep and fearsome might.
Yet we step forth, against the night,
With hopes and dreams, our guiding light.

The void beneath may call our name,
And shadows rise to stake their claim.
But we hold fast, our spirits flame,
Defying doubts that dare to maim.

Each bridge we build with love and trust,
Turns fragile dreams to iron dust.
With every step, beyond we thrust,
To forge a path from chaos' lust.

In silence vast, our courage gleams,
Reflecting all our boundless dreams.
We navigate the boundless streams,
With future truths and endless schemes.

So cross we must, with hearts so bold,
For in the depths, our fate is told.
With every leap, our tale unfolds,
A testament to souls consoled.

Forged in Adversity

From fiery trials, we emerge,
With tempered will, our spirits surge.
Each hardship faced, each anguished urge,
In strength and grace, we then converge.

The anvil strikes of fate's cruel hand,
Shall shape our souls to bravely stand.
As mountains rise from shifting sand,
Our mettle forged by life's demand.

In storms of doubt, we plant our seed,
With resilience as our creed.
Through whispered fears, we humbly lead,
For in our hearts, the truth we heed.

Each scar and wound, a tale retold,
Of battles fought, of courage bold.
In darkest nights, our fires enfold,
A legacy of dreams upheld.

Though trials come and pain may thrive,
It's through adversity we strive.
For in our hearts, we keep alive,
The strength that helps us, to survive.

Rising Tide

Beneath the moon's reflective gaze,
The ocean swells in mystic haze.
With rhythms old as ancient days,
It calls to us in gentle praise.

The rising tide, a force of might,
Emerging from the depths of night.
It sweeps away both fear and fright,
And carries dreams to newfound height.

In harmony, the waves align,
A symphony of pure design.
With every crest, a sign divine,
Of life reborn through fate's entwine.

Upon the shore, with open hearts,
We greet the dawn as night departs.
In unity, our journey starts,
As one with nature's flawless arts.

So let the ocean's whispers guide,
As we embrace the rising tide.
Together strong, we shall abide,
And sail beyond the worlds we hide.

Under Unyielding Skies

Beneath the heavens' weight, I stand,
My dreams are etched in shifting sands.
Bound by stars that never wane,
In twilight's grasp, I chase the flame.

A whisper carried on the breeze,
Tales of love that bring me ease.
The moon, a guardian of night,
Guides my heart with silver light.

Shadows stretch and shadows fall,
Upon this earth, I heed the call.
With every step, a path unfolds,
A journey's tale in stories told.

Mountains rise and rivers flow,
Under skies, my spirit grows.
Within each storm, a spark ignites,
A beacon burning through the nights.

Eyes that seek the sun's embrace,
Heartbeats echoing in space.
With courage drawn from endless skies,
I rise once more, to endless tries.

Emerging from the Deep

In oceans dark, where shadows creep,
A silent world where secrets sleep.
From depths of blue, I fight to rise,
Towards the light of open skies.

Currents strong, they pull me near,
But hope remains, a steadfast seer.
Through waves of doubt, I move ahead,
By inner light, my path is led.

Mirrored dreams in waters clear,
Reflections of what I hold dear.
Through silent realms, my heart ascends,
To realms above, where struggles end.

Whispers of the sea's embrace,
Caress my soul, a gentle grace.
With each pulse, a purpose found,
In ocean's depths, where I am bound.

From the abyss, I make my way,
Emerging strong, to greet the day.
With every breath, I rise anew,
Eternal tides that guide me through.

Seeds of Persistence

In barren soil, a seed is sown,
Amidst the earth, where dreams are grown.
With patience, sun, and tender care,
A life begins, a hope to share.

Though winds may howl and rains may fall,
Each trial faced, a call to all.
Roots dig deep, defy the storm,
In struggle's wake, new forms are born.

Leaves unfold with morning's light,
A testament to endless fight.
From fragile sprout to towering tree,
A symbol of resilience, free.

Branches stretch towards the sky,
A dance of life, where spirits fly.
In every bud, a future blooms,
A promise held in nature's womb.

With every season, growth revealed,
In times of drought, in fields once sealed.
Seeds of persistence, hearts maintain,
A story told in sun and rain.

Rise From Ashes

In fire's realm, where ashes lay,
A silent vow begins the day.
From embers cold, a spark will grow,
To light the path that none could know.

The past consumed in flames' embrace,
Yet strength emerges, finds its place.
Through trials harsh, a heart repeats,
A journey born on burning streets.

With every loss, a lesson learned,
In phoenix flames, a spirit burned.
The ash beneath, a fertile ground,
For rebirth in the silence found.

Wings unfurl in dawn's first light,
A testament to endless night.
From shadows deep, I rise anew,
A journey forged in what is true.

Heartbeats echo, strong and clear,
A rhythm born of conquered fear.
In every fall, a rise ensured,
A testament to life endured.

The Unseen Path

Through forests dense where shadows play,
In twilight's soft and fleeting gray,
An unseen path begins to weave,
With secrets whispers barely leave.

The fallen leaves, a tapestry,
Of countless steps in memory,
Each whispering wind a hidden call,
Guiding souls both brave and small.

Between the trees where moonlight dips,
In silver streams and slender slips,
The journey winds and seldom clear,
Yet footsteps echo, growing near.

To travel where the heart does lead,
With courage as your only creed,
The unseen path, a tale untold,
In every footfall, marked in gold.

Mountains high and valleys deep,
Through dreams and while the world sleeps,
The path unseen by naked eye,
Embraces those who dare to try.

Invisible Armor

In battles fought within the mind,
A strength unknown, yet well-defined,
Invisible armor, firm and bright,
Guards the heart throughout the night.

With every thought, a shield is born,
Through whispers mild and tempests torn,
Against the dark, this light will stand,
Invisible, yet close at hand.

The fears that clasp with icy grip,
Are turned away with wisdom's tip,
And courage, unseen guards the gate,
Protecting soul from cruel fate.

Though frailties may oft appear,
Invisible armor, sharp and clear,
Deflects the arrows of despair,
In fights unseen, it is aware.

When hope seems but a distant gleam,
Remember this enduring theme,
Invisible armor girds the soul,
Helping hearts to stay whole.

Unshattered Dream

In quiet nights when silence grows,
A dream unshattered softly flows,
Through starlit skies, with whispers low,
To realms where only dreamers go.

In slumber's grasp, the visions bloom,
Escaping from the tight-spun loom,
Of daily cares and waking strives,
Into a world where hope revives.

Each thread of light, a beacon true,
Guiding hearts where spirits flew,
Beyond the reach of time's embrace,
To places filled with boundless grace.

Awaking not to shattered ties,
But to a dawn with softened skies,
Where dreams align with waking sight,
And morning brings a fresh delight.

Hold fast to every dream you weave,
In waking hours they never leave,
Unshattered by the world outside,
They flourish where your heart resides.

Journey's End

At last the road comes to a rest,
With sunset painting skies in zest,
A journey long with tales amassed,
Now finds its end in peace at last.

The steps that echoed through the years,
Leave trails of joy and trails of tears,
Yet every path and winding turn,
Led to the moment we now discern.

The miles behind, a tapestry,
Of lessons learned in memory,
Each star above, a guiding light,
Reflecting on the past fought fight.

In silence now, the traveler stands,
With open heart and open hands,
Grateful for the winding road,
And each new dawn that it bestowed.

Though journeys end, another nears,
With faith and hope and fleeting fears,
For every end's a start anew,
Of paths unseen, awaiting you.

Sailing Against Tempests

Amidst the ocean's raging cry,
We brave the stormy, endless sky.
With hearts determined, spirits high,
We steer the ship, no fear nor sigh.

Dark clouds gather, waves do rise,
Yet hope reflects in sailors' eyes.
The tempest roars, but so do we,
Chasing dreams on the wild sea.

Each gust a test, each swell a dare,
Our souls undaunted, truth laid bare.
We sail through thunder's fierce embrace,
In every storm, we find our grace.

Stars above, though veiled and shy,
Guide us through night's lullaby.
With firm resolve, we pierce the dark,
Our voyage etched with fate's own mark.

We navigate tempestuous night,
Towards the dawn, we set our sight.
For in the tempest's daunting dance,
We find our strength, our valiant chance.

Skyward Bound

Through realms of clouds, our spirits soar,
Above life's trials, evermore.
With wings of hope, we leave the ground,
To where the stars in silence sound.

The heavens call with whispered grace,
We chase the dreams through endless space.
Beneath the moon's soft, tender glow,
Infinite possibilities flow.

Boundless skies and endless blue,
Reflect the paths we dare pursue.
Among the constellations bright,
Our aims take flight in wondrous light.

Against the wind, our hearts beat true,
In quest of dreams both old and new.
Skyward bound with courage bold,
Through skies uncharted, dreams unfold.

We let the starlight guide us high,
Beyond the limits of the sky.
In every cloud, horizon bound,
We find the peace once lost but found.

Unveiling Dawn

In the hush before the light,
Where darkness kisses dawn goodnight,
A tender promise softly wakes,
As morning's breath the silence breaks.

Through the veil of night, it peers,
Dispelling shadows, calming fears.
The first light's whisper graces all,
As sunlight climbs the sky's great hall.

Colors burst from night's embrace,
Painting skies with rosy grace.
Each ray a stroke of warmth and cheer,
A masterpiece both bright and clear.

Birds sing praises to the morn,
In melodies of day reborn.
Their harmonies in chorus weave,
A testament of dreams achieved.

With dawn unveiled, new hope ignites,
Hearts awakened by its light.
As day unfolds its vibrant span,
Embrace the dawn, the endless plan.

Phoenix in the Rain

Beneath the storm, where shadows tread,
A flame ignites despite the dread.
From ashes cold, it rises grand,
A phoenix bold in rain's command.

Amidst the drops, it spreads its wings,
Defying fate that sorrow brings.
Resilient heart and spirit bright,
It soars beyond the darkest night.

Raindrops fall, yet fire remains,
In every tear, a spark sustains.
The phoenix dances in the storm,
In every trial, its strength reborn.

Through thunder's roar and lightning's glare,
It finds its path with fearless flair.
With every flame, it sheds the past,
Emerging from the storm steadfast.

In rain it finds a kindred soul,
Both cleansing fire and water's role.
As phoenix rises, so do we,
In life's great storm, forever free.

Tides of Courage

In shadows deep, the heart does quake,
Yet in the dark, resolve we make.
The ocean's might, it ebbs, it flows,
With every wave, the courage grows.

Upon the shore, where dreams collide,
We face the fears we cannot hide.
The salty spray, the seagull's cry,
A testament to days gone by.

The moon above, it draws the sea,
As courage draws out bravery.
In tidal dance, we find our way,
Through nights of fear to light of day.

For every storm, a dawn will break,
And with it, strength we cannot fake.
Tides of courage, fierce and wild,
Nurture within, a warrior child.

Shattered, Yet Whole

Broken shards upon the ground,
In silence, they make mournful sound.
Each fragment holds a tale, a name,
Of love and loss, of joy and shame.

From hopeless wreck, a phoenix soars,
Amidst the ruins, new hope restores.
The shattered self becomes the art,
A mosaic made from each small part.

In cracks, the light begins to swirl,
Revealing beauty in the whirl.
Imperfections mark life's toll,
Yet through them, we become whole.

The ghost of pain, a bittersweet,
In memory, our hearts do meet.
From brokenness, a strength appears,
A legacy of conquered fears.

Embracing the Struggle

The path untrod, with thorn and stone,
In solitude, we walk alone.
Each burden carried on the back,
In struggle, we find what we lack.

The night is long, the journey cold,
Yet in the trials, true grit is bold.
With every step, our souls ignite,
For in the dark, we find the light.

Mountains high, with peaks afar,
We measure worth by every scar.
In valleys low, where shadows creep,
Our strength awakens from the deep.

To embrace the struggle is to grow,
And in adversity, we glow.
Our spirit forged in heat and strife,
A testimony to the life.

Conquering the Unseen

In realms of thought, where shadows play,
We battle fears that find their way.
Invisible, they shapeless form,
Yet in our hearts, they rage a storm.

The mind's deceit, it twists and turns,
In unseen lairs, where darkness burns.
But in the quiet, truth is found,
Our inner strength, it stands its ground.

With whispered words, the courage breeds,
In darkest hours, it plants its seeds.
The battles fought within our soul,
Are victories that make us whole.

The unseen foes, they lose their might,
In dawn's embrace, a softer light.
For in our hearts, a beacon glows,
Conquering fears as courage grows.

Conquering Fear

Beneath the shroud of darkest night,
A heart will tremble, lose its flight,
Yet whispers come, through dreams alight,
To show the path, and grant new sight.

A thunder's clash, it shakes the air,
The challenge met, with strength to spare,
In shadows deep, but still aware,
The courage blooms, despite despair.

Each stride is bold, each breath is clear,
To silence doubt, and quell the tear,
Through tempest wild, the way we steer,
In every pulse, we conquer fear.

With lantern high, and mind serene,
The spirit shines, in twilight's sheen,
No longer bound by cords unseen,
As fear dissolves, the soul's redeem.

A dawn will break, on valleys wide,
The heart unleashed, with newfound pride,
From chains of dusk, we now abide,
In freedom's light, we stride inside.

Dusk to Dawn

As twilight falls, and shadows grow,
The world adorned, in amber glow,
A sleepy hush, the night will know,
Where whispers soft, and dreams will flow.

Stars alight, in heavens wide,
A cosmic quilt, our souls confide,
With lunar beams, as guide and tide,
The darkened waves, we'll gently ride.

Silent skies, in velvet drape,
The worlds unseen, begin to shape,
From dusk's embrace, no path to escape,
On whispered winds, the dreams will cape.

In tranquil nights, the secrets blend,
Where midnight tales, and wishes send,
A tender hope, to hearts we lend,
Till breaking dawn, the night will mend.

And as the sun begins its rise,
The night dissolves, in morning's eyes,
From starlit dreams, to day's reprise,
From dusk to dawn, our spirits rise.

Shattering Barriers

A wall stands tall, a mighty brink,
Yet courage flows, through every link,
With steadfast will, no fear to shrink,
The barriers quake, and start to sink.

Each challenge faced, with fervent might,
Through shadows cast, we'll seek the light,
A journey bold, to claims of right,
We pierce the dark, and scale the height.

No chain can hold, no gate confine,
The heart that beats, with pulse divine,
In every step, our strength align,
To shatter bounds, and freely shine.

The echoes roll, and mountains quiver,
With iron will, we cross the river,
For dreams that blaze, will make us shiver,
But in their heat, we won't deliver.

Together strong, our paths reveal,
The power felt, so bold and real,
Through broken walls, our spirits heal,
In shattering barriers, we make the deal.

From Within

A quiet seed, so deep inside,
In shadows hides, where doubts reside,
Yet warmth and light, the fears will bide,
To spark the flame, and light the stride.

A whisper soft, a voice so true,
It stirs the soul, in morning dew,
With strength of heart, and worldly view,
From within, the life renew.

Through valleys low, and mountains high,
The inward spark, will never die,
In every tear, and every sigh,
From within, the dreams will fly.

In stillness found, the silence speaks,
With echo's sound, the spirit seeks,
A voyage deep, where meaning peaks,
From within, the guidance leaks.

And as we grow, and truths we glean,
The inward light, will ever sheen,
From shadows dark, to loves unseen,
From within, the world is clean.

Above the Maelstrom

Waves that crash but never cease,
Whispers rise within the breeze.
Hearts aflame, a wild release,
Lifted up, despite unease.

Storms may roar and skies may weep,
Yet above, the dreams don't sleep.
Through the tempest, spirits leap,
Into peace so vast and deep.

Hope's ember through the darkness fights,
Guiding through the stormy nights.
In the maelstrom, come the lights,
Above the chaos, pure delights.

Strength is found in every surge,
Voices blend, a solemn dirge.
Onward, through the waves they merge,
Finding paths where dreams emerge.

Beyond the turmoil, clear and calm,
Lies a vista, soothing balm.
In the stillness, life's a psalm,
Above the maelstrom, we are calm.

Infinite Ascent

Steps that climb without an end,
Journey of the heart to mend.
Mountains tall that softly blend,
Horizons new, around the bend.

Stars align, a path aglow,
Through the night, where winds do blow.
In the sky, our spirits grow,
Infinite ascent below.

Travelling through lands uncharted,
Every peak, a vision started.
To the heavens, dreams imparted,
With each step, we're never parted.

Whispers from the heights above,
Tell of strength and endless love.
Boundless sky, like wings of dove,
Rise as one, to realms thereof.

Through the clouds and past the gate,
Timeless realms our souls elate.
Endless journeys we create,
Infinite ascent, our fate.

Shielded by Grace

In the shadow of the night,
Light of grace is shining bright.
Heart of stone turns feather-light,
In her arms, our spirits take flight.

Whispers soft and gentle hum,
Speak of where our hope is from.
In her shelter, heartbeats drum,
Grace abounds, our fears become.

Faithful through the endless trial,
Love protects through every mile.
In her hands, we rest awhile,
Shielded by her gentle smile.

Through the storms and darkened days,
Grace will always find the ways.
Guiding us through life's mazes,
In her warmth, our souls do blaze.

Harmony in every breath,
Grace defends us, barring death.
In her light, we find our path,
Shielded by her tender wrath.

Awakening Might

Silent whispers of the dawn,
Come as dreams of night are gone.
Through the mist, a strength is drawn,
Mighty as the breaking dawn.

From the ashes, rise anew,
Awakening the power true.
In the depths, a force we knew,
Born again, our spirits flew.

Heartbeats loud, no longer tame,
Fuelled by hope, igniting flame.
Every pulse, a fierce exclaim,
Awakening might in name.

Mountains tremble at our roar,
Unleashed power evermore.
In our stride, we conquer, soar,
Spirit strong to every core.

Through the night and through the day,
Mighty hearts will find the way.
With our spirits bright and gay,
Awakening might, come what may.

Unyielding Heartbeat

In twilight's tender, fleeting glow,
A steadfast pulse does gently flow.
With every beat, the night relents,
The heart within remains content.

Through trials fierce and shadows deep,
This vibrant drum, its rhythm keeps.
An unyielding force that won't decay,
Guides the soul till break of day.

Amidst the storm's relentless song,
It carries on, both firm and strong.
A beacon through the darkest night,
Its steady thrum, a guiding light.

Each rise and fall, a tale conveyed,
Of battles fought and hopes displayed.
In silent strength, it ever beats,
A timeless cadence that repeats.

No matter where the path may bend,
This heartbeat's flame will not descend.
Through joy and pain, it perseveres,
An unyielding tune, throughout the years.

Invincible Resolve

In the quiet dawn, resolve is born,
A spark ignites, no longer worn.
With every step, a strength renewed,
Invincible, with heart imbued.

Determination, fierce and bright,
Guides through trials, day and night.
Unwavering in its command,
A steadfast grip on each demand.

Through flames and floods, it does advance,
Undeterred by circumstance.
A force that rises, never yields,
In every heart, this power heals.

With steel resolve, it carves its way,
Defying doubts that oft betray.
In every quest, it stands its ground,
In every soul, this truth is found.

Through shadows cast and daunting height,
It finds the strength to reignite.
An invincible resolve within,
To strive, to dream, to fight, to win.

Whispered Recovery

In the hush, recovery sings,
A melody on tender wings.
Soft whispers heal the deepest scars,
With gentle light from distant stars.

Through fragile moments, time will weave,
A tapestry that can't deceive.
Each whispered note, a touch so kind,
To mend the heart and ease the mind.

In silence found, where echoes meet,
A rhythm calm, a pulse discreet.
Recovery whispers sweet and low,
And through the pain, new blossoms grow.

The quiet strength of whispered care,
Renewing faith, dispelling despair.
It softly hums a lullaby,
To lift the spirit, help it fly.

In gentle waves, recovery's tide,
Will soothe and mend what's torn inside.
With whispered hope that softly breathes,
A soul reborn, a heart that seethes.

Boundless Courage

In the face of daunting fright,
A spark ignites, a flame takes flight.
Boundless courage, fierce and grand,
Strength untamed by any hand.

It rises high, defies the storm,
In every heart, it takes its form.
Through each trial, it never wanes,
Unyielding in its mighty gains.

Courage boundless, bold, and true,
Guides each step and sees us through.
With every breath, it grows in might,
A beacon shining, pure and bright.

Against the odds, it stands its ground,
In courage, endless strength is found.
In every soul, it gently burns,
A lesson learned, a truth that churns.

Through darkest night and fiercest light,
Boundless courage takes its flight.
A timeless force, a gallant creed,
The heart's true rhythm, its noble deed.

Braving the Rapids

Beneath the rushing skies so fierce,
The waters roar, their voice austere.
With oars in hand and hearts alight,
We face the dauntless, ceaseless night.

In torrents wild, where currents twist,
Our spirits rise, our fears dismissed.
Together, steadfast in the fray,
We chase the dawn, we chase the day.

The river's waltz we boldly dance,
In rippling light, in daring glance.
Through churning waves, through countless trials,
We carve our path for endless miles.

With every surge and every crest,
We forge ahead and face the test.
For in the storm's embrace, we find
The courage heart, the steely mind.

As twilight fades to morning's hue,
The tranquil streams speak of the truth:
In braving rapids, fears in tow,
We find our strength, we let it show.

Unveiling the Strength Within

In shadows deep where fear resides,
A spark begins, a light collides.
From weary nights to breaking dawn,
We rise anew, our strength reborn.

Through whispered doubts and silent screams,
We hold on fast to fragile dreams.
With every step, though trembling, small,
We conquer fear, we stand up tall.

The echoes of the past may cling,
But from within our hearts will sing.
A melody of hope's refrain,
That drowns out all the silent pain.

In moments bleak, we look inside,
And find the strength that had to hide.
We build anew from shattered clay,
And mend the cracks, we find our way.

Unseen, unheard, we find the light,
That guides us through the darkest night.
With newfound strength, we break, we bend,
And find the truth at journey's end.

Overcoming the Abyss

When shadows claim the light of day,
And hope begins to drift away,
We stand upon the edge so vast,
And face the fears that haunt the past.

In echoes of a silent cry,
We find the will to reach and try.
With every breath, we grasp the air,
And steady hearts, we do not scare.

The abyss calls with siren's plea,
A whisper dark, "Come follow me."
But light within our souls does burn,
With every step, we shall return.

Through nights of doubt and days so long,
We gather strength, we gather song.
To rise above the endless gloom,
And carve our path, dispel the doom.

The chasm wide, the leap so bold,
Yet in our hearts, the tale is told:
Of courage found and battles won,
When shadows fade beneath the sun.

Embracing the Climb

The mountain high, the peak afar,
A journey long, a guiding star.
With every step, the air grows thin,
But strength within helps us begin.

The trail is steep, the path unclear,
Yet forward tread with little fear.
Through rocky crags and winds that bind,
We press ahead with heart and mind.

In moments hard, when doubts assail,
We find resolve, we will not fail.
With every grip and foothold brief,
We garner hope, we gather belief.

With skies above and earth below,
Our spirits lift as we bestow,
A sense of pride in every stride,
For we embrace the climb with pride.

Upon the summit, view so grand,
We understand, we take our stand.
Through trials faced and heights attained,
Our spirits freed, our souls unchained.

Milton Keynes UK
Ingram Content Group UK Ltd.
UKHW022012290824
447585UK00006B/232

CHAPTER 63

When I open the door to the turret room, it's as if the intervening years have disappeared. The desks where Alice and I sat are still there facing each other. The broken window is, as it was on the night Kate died. But nothing is ever what it seems. I know that now. I'm satisfied justice was done and that I played a small part in it. If it wasn't for my husband, the wrong man would have been convicted of Kate's murder.

I open the door leading to the walkway separating Cameron's bedroom from the turret room. I can see two figures on the beach below me. My husband looks around and raises his hand then leaves his son to explore. I see him walking up the steps towards the house. The wind howls and blows through his dark hair, which like mine, is beginning to turn grey. I hear the door close and his footsteps on the stairs. I wait until he stands at my side.

"I've remembered. It *was* Finbar I saw. I thought he'd killed Kate. He was covered in blood."

Guy slips an arm around my shoulders.

"He was as much to blame as Cameron. Kate was right all along."

After the court case, I remember Guy telling me that with the help of Lance Rodway, he'd learned that Cameron Blackstone had attended a psychiatric clinic in the States after he'd attacked a colleague over a dispute at work. It was unprovoked and he was sacked over it. But it was agreed that, if he attended the clinic, the man he attacked would drop all charges. However, slowly but surely his past was catching up with him. He needed to get away from the States. And that was when he rang Finbar.

I look towards the cliff path.

"Blackstone was a clinical psychopath, able to appear the lover, the friend, the professional photographer, without raising suspicion." Guy says.

"Except for Alice," I reply looking towards her cottage where I see a child's swing in the garden.

"That was why he killed her. She knew what he was. It was as simple as that."

"I wished I'd listened to her."

"You weren't to know. None of us were." Guy holds me close. "He was responsible for Melody Cassidy's death. You know it was he who gave her the drugs and he who took her into the bedroom. Mickey Coburn thought he saw the two of them going *into* the bedroom with Melody when in fact Cameron had called Finn on his mobile and the two of them were *leaving* the room, having removed all traces of their occupancy. Cameron called the tune and Finn danced along. Remember Finn admitting it to me, after he was released."

"Alice always said it was Cameron and not Finbar who was the troublemaker. I must be a bad judge of character, first Kenneth Boysey - he took an overdose and I had to deal with the aftermath, then Cameron Blackstone – I thought I was the only one who could see the good in him." I look down at Ben who is leaning against the boathouse. He is nearly twelve now and sees his father as often as he can. My marriage is good; we love each other, "This time I'm lucky."

"That's for sure, you have nothing to worry about on that score and as for the other two you don't need to feel guilty about a thing." His kiss is warm on my cheek. "When you gave me the sovereign and chain belonging to Finn and told me where you found it, I couldn't quite believe he had the courage to commit murder, in spite of the circumstantial evidence. As it turned out I was right. But I do believe he knew Cameron killed Alice

Phillips. And who knows, he might have been indirectly involved. If there's one thing I know about my ex brother-in-law, he was as weak as a wet dishcloth."

He frowns and I can see how hard it is for him, remembering it all again.

"I shouldn't have put you through this."

"Nonsense, this will put an end to it, once and for all. I always felt that Blackstone was obsessed with Kate from the minute he first saw her. But I was wrapped up in work at the time and Kate had many admirers; I just thought he was another one. Finn was initially the catalyst who brought them together but it didn't turn out as Blackstone initially intended."

He shivers as a gust of wind blows along the walkway. "Looking back, I realise, his whole agenda was to discredit Finn. He never forgave him for marrying Kate. He tried to make you believe that Finn was responsible for poisoning you with the headache pills. However, his real intention was to put doubt and fear in *Kate's* mind regarding Finn, but it backfired."

"So that was why he asked me to watch what I ate? I know we've discussed this before but it all seems so much more real now."

"Exactly. Remember, he even tried to shift the

blame for the murders on to Finn's shoulders, so much so that the police took him in for questioning but there was no real evidence linking him to either of them."

"But there could have been - if I'd remembered seeing him on the stairs."

"Don't think about it. It didn't happen. As for Blackstone, I'm sure the argument, that led him to murder Kate, began with him implying Finn was responsible for Alice's death but knowing Kate she'd have just laughed at him and told him that he wasn't capable of doing such a thing."

"But you were the one who made the difference with the evidence you'd collected in the States. If it hadn't been for you, Cameron Blackstone would have been released. I don't want to think about how it might have turned out; it's one step too far."

I watch the swirling currents in the bay and remember how Cameron and I had been tossed into the depths on the Cobblestones. He couldn't have been all bad or he wouldn't have saved me. I close my eyes; sympathy for a cold-blooded murderer is a wasted emotion. No doubt Alice had been right, he was being watched from the shore, it wasn't as if we were alone. Perhaps his intention had been to place my death on Finbar's shoulders also; he kept telling everyone that he'd rented the boat from one of Finn's dodgy friends. He must have known it wasn't exactly seaworthy and he definitely knew I wasn't a strong swimmer, after all he'd seen me get into difficulties once before.

It was reported that Finbar was drunk when he tried to take the yacht out and that the Cobblestone currents were too much for him but I see things differently. He was never much of a swimmer and was aware the boat needed repairing. I believe he knew exactly what he was doing. Laura Crighton and Steward Grant's pictures were splashed all over the tabloid newspapers. Their marriage was reported on every news channel. There was nothing left for him and I think he took the coward's way out. He'd spent too long under Cameron's influence that without him he was adrift like a ship without a sail.

"Come along, you're shivering. We've seen enough." Guy steers me back towards the staircase. As we turn the corner, a shaft of sunlight shoots through the stained glass window blinding me but I lean on my husband's arm as he guides me towards the light.

The End.

ABOUT THE AUTHOR

K.J.Rabane's main interest is in writing psychological thrillers. She also works as a supporting artist for film and television and lives in Penarth, near Cardiff, South Wales. Details of this book, together with her other eBooks, can be found by visiting her web page.

www.kjrabane.co.uk.

Printed in Great Britain
by Amazon.co.uk, Ltd.,
Marston Gate.